Cambridge English Readers
· ·
Starter Level

Series editor: Philip Prowse

Let Me Out!

Antoinette Moses

CAMBRIDGE
UNIVERSITY PRESS

CAMBRIDGE UNIVERSITY PRESS

Cambridge, New York, Melbourne, Madrid, Cape Town, Singapore, São Paulo, Delhi

Cambridge University Press
The Edinburgh Building, Cambridge CB2 8RU, UK

www.cambridge.org
Information on this title: www.cambridge.org/9780521683296

First published 2006
5th printing 2007

Antoinette Moses has asserted her right to be identified as the Author of the Work in
accordance with the Copyright, Design and Patents Act 1988.

Printed in Italy by Legoprint S.p.A

Illustrations by Chris Pavely

A catalogue record for this book is available from the British Library

ISBN 978-0-521-68329-6 paperback
ISBN 978-0-521-68330-2 paperback plus audio CD pack

Contents

Chapter 1   My name is Nolan   5
Chapter 2   I can do anything   9
Chapter 3   Not just a robot   15
Chapter 4   I'm not funny   18
Chapter 5   Goodbye, Sam   23
Chapter 6   Let me out!   27

People in the story

 **John** is 30. He lives in an apartment with his dog. He makes robots.

 **Nolan** is a robot.

 **Sam** is John's dog.

 **Mr. Peters** works with John. He has the money.

Chapter 1 *My name is Nolan*

'I am. Yes. But what am I?'

There's something in front of me. It's a tall thing.

'Hi! Can you hear me?' The tall thing makes a noise. It speaks. I understand that. I can understand things. I understand that the tall thing speaks and I can understand what it says.

'I can hear you,' I say. I can speak too. I'm speaking.

'Great! Great! This is great!' says the tall thing. He changes his face. This is a smile. I don't know how I know it's a smile, but I know. He's smiling at me. He's very happy. I know this too. A smile = happy.

'Great. You can understand me. Hello,' says the tall thing. 'OK. I'm John and you're my robot. Can you say that?'

'I'm John and you're my robot,' I say.

'No,' says John. He does something on his computer.

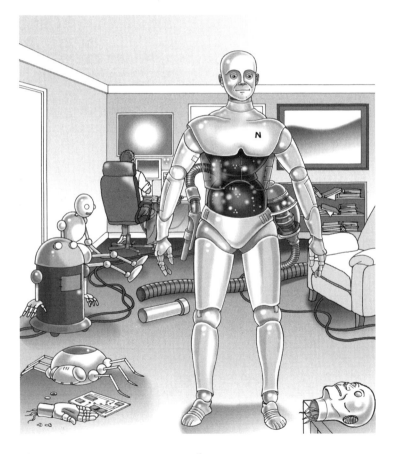

I understand the word 'computer'. There's a computer in my head. The computer teaches me English.

'You're John and I'm your robot,' I say. 'You're happy and I'm great.'

'Good, good,' says John. 'This is great. I'm going to be famous.'

'You're going to be famous,' I say. 'Am I going to be famous?' I ask.

'Of course you're going to be famous,' says John. 'You're going to be famous and I'm going to be very rich.'

'Am I going to be rich?' I ask.

'No, you can't be rich,' says John. 'You're just a robot. You can't have money.'

I don't like this. I want money. I want to be famous *and* rich. But I don't say anything.

'Can I have a name?' I ask. 'You're John, but who am I?'

John looks at me. Then he sees there are words on my arm. They say:

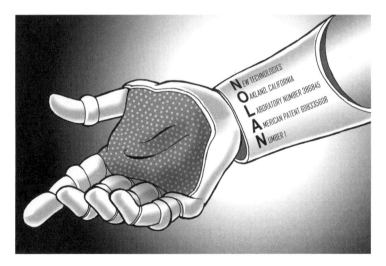

'Your name is Nolan,' says John.
'I'm Nolan,' I say. 'Hi, John. Meet Nolan.'
'Hi, Nolan,' says John. 'Nice to meet you.'

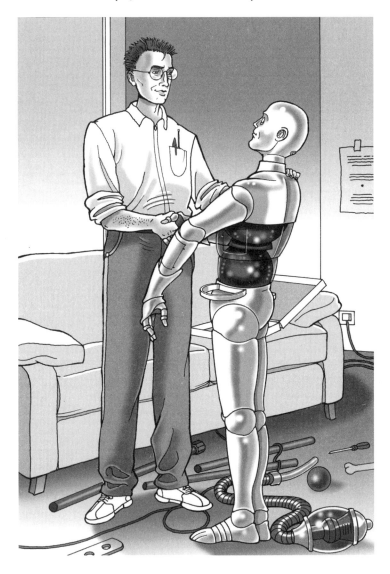

Chapter 2 *I can do anything*

John lives in a small apartment. It has four rooms: the living room, the bedroom, a kitchen and a bathroom. It's a nice apartment, but it's dirty. John is always working. He doesn't clean the apartment.

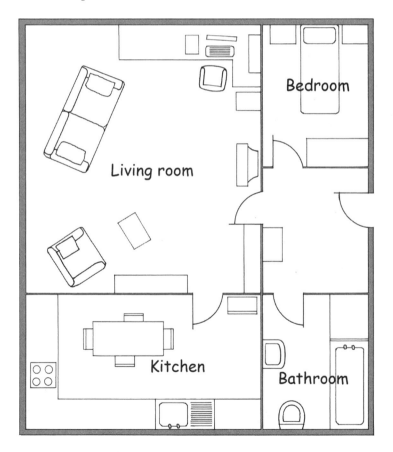

'OK, Nolan,' says John. 'Now you can help me. You can clean my apartment.'

'OK, John,' I say. My English is very good now. I clean the kitchen and the bathroom. I clean the living room and the bedroom. John is very happy. I am happy. I like cleaning John's apartment.

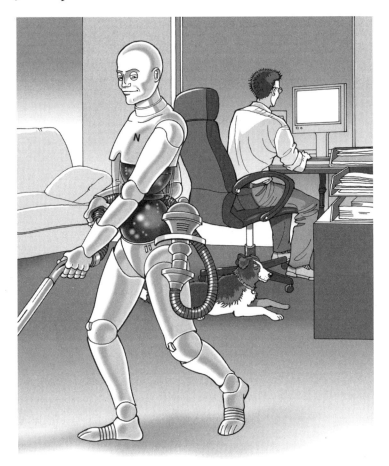

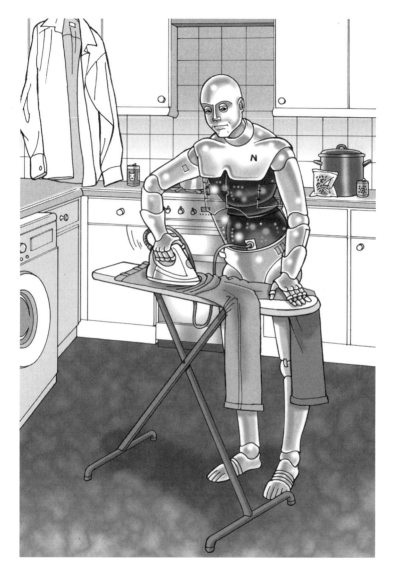

Every day I clean John's apartment. I wash his jeans and shirts in the washing machine. I iron his jeans and shirts. I make his food.

'You're great, Nolan,' says John. 'You can do anything.'

I can do anything.

I control the apartment. I can open the doors and the windows and I can close the doors and the windows. At night I lock the doors. Then no-one can get in. I can make things go on and go off. I can control the iron. This makes the clothes flat and nice. But I can't control the dog. I tell the dog things, but the dog doesn't do them.

'Clean the kitchen,' I say to the dog. But the dog doesn't do anything.

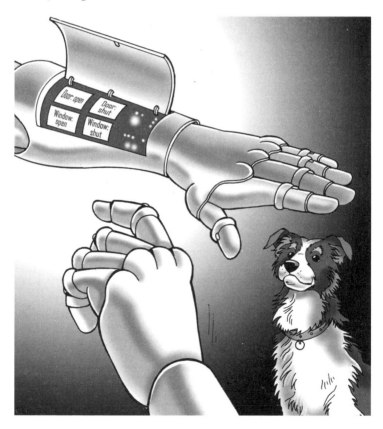

The dog has a name. He's called Sam.

Sam doesn't work but I work all the time. I like working. Sam sits and walks and eats. John likes Sam. I don't understand this. The dog is wrong. He doesn't work well. I work very well.

In the evening John goes out and Sam goes with him. At eleven o'clock John and Sam come home. I hear them. I open the door. John laughs; he's happy. Sam likes going out. He's happy, but he doesn't laugh.

I never go out with John. John never asks me. I'm not happy. I open doors. I close doors. I can make John laugh. I can do anything, but John never takes me out. He never asks me to go with him. He takes Sam. I don't like Sam.

Chapter 3 *Not just a robot*

I'm in the kitchen with Sam. Sam makes a big noise because he's afraid of me. John comes in.

'What is it?' he asks Sam. 'Are you afraid of Nolan? Come here. Good dog, Sam. Nolan is just a robot.'

Sam goes to John and John is very nice to him.

'Sam's a bad dog,' I say.

John laughs. 'Sam doesn't understand robots. He thinks you're a boy. He doesn't like boys.'

'Sam must go,' I say.

'Sam can't go,' John says. 'I love Sam. He's my family.'

'I'm your family,' I say.

'You're just a robot,' laughs John.

'Why am I just a robot?' I ask.

'Because you are,' says John. 'Because … because you aren't a person. You … you can't feel.'

'I can feel happy,' I tell him.

'Can you?' asks John. 'Can you feel sad?' John asks me.

'What is sad?' I ask.

'Sad is …? How can I tell a robot? Sad is … My mother and father are dead. I think about them and I'm sad,' says John. 'And I'm sad because I don't have a brother or sister. And because I don't have many friends.'

'Why don't you have many friends?' I ask him.

'People don't understand my work,' he says. 'They don't understand how interesting robots are.'

'Am I interesting?' I ask.

'Yes, Nolan,' he says. 'You're very interesting. You're my life's work.'

'Is Sam interesting?' I ask.

'No,' John tells me. 'Sam isn't interesting. He's a dog.'

I don't understand. 'But you love Sam,' I say.

'Yes,' says John. 'I love Sam.'

'And you don't love me?' I ask.

'Why am I having this conversation with a robot?' asks John. 'Nolan, you're not a person. I can't love you.'

'You can't love me because I don't feel,' I say.

'No,' says John. 'Well, yes.'

John is wrong. I'm not just a robot. I *can* feel. I feel angry. I can hate. I hate Sam. Sam must go.

Chapter 4 *I'm not funny*

Sam must go. I put him out and he comes in again. I control this apartment, but I can't control him.

It's the next morning. A man is here in my home. John tells him things. 'Nolan can do anything,' says John.

'Clean the apartment,' John says to me.

'It's ten o'clock in the morning,' I say. 'I make coffee at ten o'clock. I clean the apartment at ten thirty.'

'Just do it, Nolan,' says John. His face is red; he looks angry. 'Clean the apartment, Nolan. This is Mr. Peters. He's going to watch.' Mr. Peters laughs. I don't like Mr. Peters.

'OK,' I say. I clean the room.

'This is very interesting,' says Mr. Peters.

'Now I'm going to clean the dog,' I say.

'Nolan, I don't think this is a good …' John says. But I have water. I put the water on Sam.

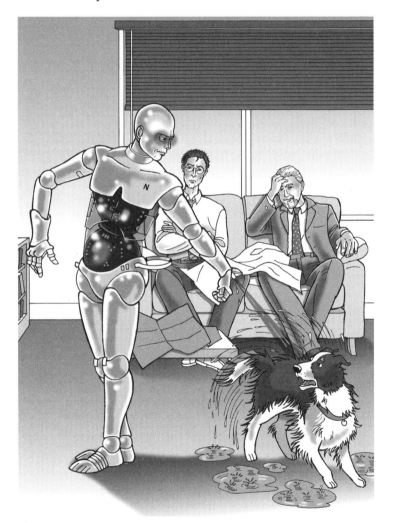

Sam makes a big noise and runs out of the room.

'Stop!' I shout. Sam doesn't stop. There's a lot of water on the floor and Mr. Peters is laughing again.

'Why are you laughing?' I ask Mr. Peters.

'Your robot's very funny, John,' says Mr. Peters.

'I'm not funny,' I say. 'I'm a good robot. I can do anything.'

Mr. Peters laughs and laughs. And now John is laughing.

I'm not laughing. I'm not working. I must work. Work makes me happy.

'Now I'm going to make the coffee,' I say. 'The coffee is late, but the apartment is clean.'

I go into the kitchen. I can hear John and Mr. Peters. They're laughing and laughing. I don't like it. I'm a good robot. I work all the time.

Sam is in the kitchen. I look at Sam. John loves Sam, but John thinks I'm funny. I'm not funny. John must understand. I'm going to do something. Sam is going to die.

Chapter 5 *Goodbye, Sam*

How is Sam going to die?

It isn't easy. Sam is big and I can't control him. Then I know. Sam loves cookies.

'Are you a good dog?' John asks Sam. 'Then you can have a cookie.' He gives Sam cookies.

I wait. John goes out. I open the door for him and close the door after him.

'Thank you, Nolan,' calls John.

'That's OK, John,' I say.

I go into the kitchen and find the cookies. I open the kitchen window. It's a big window.

'Sam!' I call. 'Sam! Good dog. Come here, Sam! Cookies!'

I'm standing next to the window. I have the cookies. Sam runs into the room.

'Cookies, Sam,' I say. Sam wants the cookies. He comes to me. He's now next to the window.

'Goodbye, Sam,' I say. Sam goes out of the window. He goes down. I can see him.

People come. They're shouting. Then I see John. He's running. He's running and shouting.

'Sam! Sam!' he shouts.

John is crying and shouting. Then he looks up and he sees me. He isn't laughing now. He doesn't think I'm funny now.

John comes up to the apartment. Is he angry? No. He isn't shouting. He's crying. Sam is in his arms.

'The apartment is clean,' I say. 'The dog is dirty. The dog must go out.'

'No,' says John. He looks at me. 'I'm sorry,' he says, 'but there's something wrong with you, Nolan.'

'There's nothing wrong with me,' I say. 'I'm a very good robot. The apartment is very clean.'

'You make me afraid, Nolan,' says John. 'I don't understand. I don't understand you. But you must stop.'

'I can't stop,' I say. 'I must work. Now I must make your coffee.'

'No,' says John slowly. 'I must stop you.'

Then I understand. I'm not going to be. I'm going to die. I don't want to die. I must stop John now.

'No, John,' I say. 'I must stop *you*. I can't die. *You* must die.'

Chapter 6   *Let me out!*

John takes Sam into the bathroom. I close the bathroom door and lock it. John is now in the bathroom with his dog. John is going to die there.

I go into the kitchen. There's a faucet which stops all the water. I close the faucet. Now John has no food and no water.

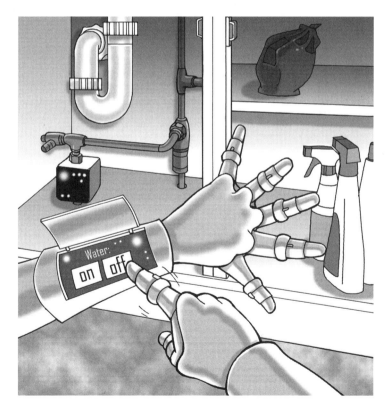

John is shouting. I don't like that. People are going to hear the noise and come here. I don't want people here. This is my apartment now. I control it.

'Let me out!' shouts John.

'I'm sorry, John,' I say. 'I can't open the door. I don't want to die.'

'You're not going to die,' says John. 'Nolan! Listen to me!'

'I'm listening,' I say.

'I'm sorry, Nolan,' says John. 'I love you. You're a great robot.'

'No,' I say. 'I'm just a robot. You think I'm funny. You love Sam.'

John is crying now. 'Please open the door, Nolan,' he says. 'I'm going to die here.'

'Yes,' I say. 'You have no food and no water. You're going to die.'

'Please, Nolan!' cries John.

'Goodbye, John,' I say.

'But you're my robot,' John says. 'What are you going to do without me?'

'I don't know,' I say. 'But I can't stop. I must go on. So you must die. Sorry, John.'

But John doesn't say anything.

So I wait. Waiting is OK. I can clean the apartment lots of times.

I wait for five days, then I go into the bathroom. John is on the floor. I put him into the bath. Then I put water into the bath. Now Sam and John are clean. I'm a very good robot.

Then I make coffee, but there's no-one here. That isn't good. I must have a new John. Then I can make him coffee. And I can clean his apartment. And I can wash his jeans and iron his shirts. He's going to love me.

*   *   *

'Hi! My name's Nolan. Nice to meet you. I'm a very good robot. Can I come home with you?'

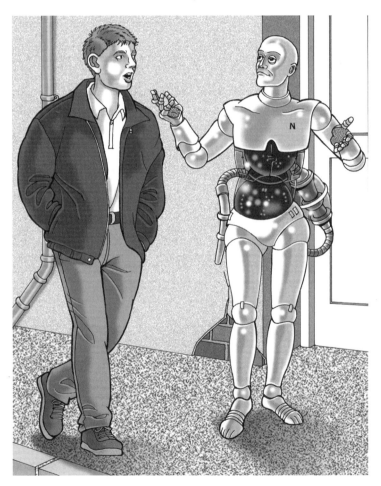

Cambridge English Readers

Look out for these other titles at the new Starter level:

The Penang File
by Richard MacAndrew
The English Prince is in Penang, Malaysia. But so is Sergio, and Sergio wants to kill him. Can Ian Munro find Sergio before it is too late?

ISBN-13 978-0-521-68331-9 paperback
ISBN-10 0-521-68331-9 paperback
ISBN-13 978-0-521-68332-6 paperback plus audio CD
ISBN-10 0-521-68332-7 paperback plus audio CD

What a Lottery!
by Colin Campbell
Rick loves music and wants to be a rock star. But he has no money and his wife leaves him. Then he wins the lottery. Is this the start of a new life for Rick?

ISBN-13 978-0-521-68327-2 paperback
ISBN-10 0-521-68327-0 paperback
ISBN-13 978-0-521-68328-9 paperback plus audio CD
ISBN-10 0-521-68328-9 paperback plus audio CD

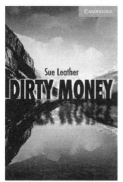

Dirty Money
by Sue Leather
Joe and Sandy love their new life in Canada. But everything changes when Pan Global come to town. Can Joe find out what the new mine is really for?

ISBN-13 978-0-521-68333-3 paperback
ISBN-10 0-521-68333-5 paperback
ISBN-13 978-0-521-68334-0 paperback plus audio CD
ISBN-10 0-521-68334-3 paperback plus audio CD

Or try these other stories by Antoinette Moses, author of
Let Me Out!

John Doe (Level 1)
The man they call John Doe lies in a hospital bed. He watches and thinks but says nothing. The doctor wants to know who he is. But John Doe doesn't answer his questions. Then, after John Doe leaves hospital, the doctor finds out more about him than just his real name.

ISBN-13 978-0-521-65619-1 paperback
ISBN-10 0-521-65619-2 paperback
ISBN-13 978-0-521-79493-0 paperback plus audio CD
ISBN-10 0-521-79493-5 paperback plus audio CD

Jojo's Story (Level 2)
'There aren't any more days. There's just time. Time when it's dark and time when it's light. Everything is dead, so why not days too?' Everyone in Jojo's village is dead, and ten-year-old Jojo is alone.

ISBN-13 978-0-521-79754-2 paperback
ISBN-10 0-521-79754-3 paperback
ISBN-13 978-0-521-68645-7 paperback plus audio CD
ISBN-10 0-521-68645-8 paperback plus audio CD

www.cambridge.org/elt/readers